JN410146

회상의 날개

The Wings of Reminiscence

Rm 210 Seoktap officetel Building
53 gil 18, Hyoryoung-ro, Seocho-gu, Seoul,
The Republic of Korea.
Telephone ; 82-2-588-4671~2
Facsimile ; 82-2-588-4673
E-mail ; hyunwoot@hanmail.net
ISBN ; 978-89-97815-31-9
Price ; USD 15.70 / 20,000won
Published in March, 20, 2024
Printed in the Republic of Korea

정찬우 한·영 대역시집
Poems of Chan-Woo Chung : A New Collection

회상의 날개
The Wings of Reminiscence

시 · 정찬우(鄭燦宇)
Written by Chan-Woo Chung; Poet, MBA

번역 · 최홍규(崔鴻圭)
Translated by Hongkyu Choe; Poet, Ph.D.

밀레
Millennium

서문

2024년도 벌써 3월 5일이 지났다

흐르는 세월을 잡을 수 없고
시대의 변화를 따를 수 없는 세상
살아 천년 죽어 천년이라는
불멸의 작품을 쓰고자
사상과 철학을 논해 보지만
헛바퀴만 도는 인생인가 보다

그럼에도 자학(子瘧)과 자해(字解)의
버릇을 버리지 못하고
또 다시 용기와 끼를 부려본다

독자들의 사랑과 우정에 감사를 드리며
가혹한 채찍과 함께 사려 깊은 마음으로
음미해주길 바란다.

2024. 3. 20.
우면산 기슭에서
의석 정찬우

Preface of The Eighth Selected Poems

In the New Year of 2024
March monthes already have passed

We stop neither time and tide
Nor follow changes of the age
As my lifetime is one thousand years
And after death is another thousand years
I wish to write imperishable poems
Dispute thoughts and philosophy
I seems that they turn around vainly

Nevertheless I don't get through completely
The habit of self-torment and self-explanation
I again courageously write in large characters

I thank readers for there love and friendship
And wish that they appreciate
With a thoughtful heart
And redoubtable whipping.

March, 20, 2024.
At the Euiseok Library near the foot of
Mt, Woomyun Seocho-gu, Seoul, Korea.
Euiseok Chan-Woo Chung, MBA.

목차

chapter 1 Night Stars in the Milky Way

제2부 그대의 모습

chapter 2 Your Shape

제3부 꿈길에서

chapter 3 On the Way of a Dream

제4부 둥둥 섬에서

chapter 4 Dungdung Isle in Seoul

제5부 바다의 초상

chapter 5 The Portrait of Sea

❖동영상 시(詩) 감상하기

youtube(유튜브)에서 '의석 정찬우'로 들어가면 150여 편의 시(詩)와 노래가 흐르는 동영상을 감상할 수 있습니다.

❖오디오 북

www.audiorac.kr

키워드 입력하기에 '정찬우'하면 현재 5권의 책이 등록되어 있습니다.

* 「내게 사랑 하나 있네(There is a Love for Me)」
* 「꽃으로 선 당신(You Stand Like A Flower)」
* 「가끔은 이런 날이(Sometimes This Day)」
* 「황홀한 여정(A Fascinating Journey)」
* 「하늘은 내게(The Heaven Is To Me)」

제1부

은하의 별밤
Night Stars in the Milky Way

시인이여

시인은 고독과 사색의 공간에 집을 짓고
외로움과 명상의 밥을 먹으며
철학과 명예에 목을 매어
존재하는 삶

하여
시인은 벗기고 벗겨도
남을게 없는 무소유의 존재이며

입힐수록 입혀지는
유소유(有所有)의 지성(知性)이다

A Poet

A poet builds his house
On the space of solitude and thinking
He eats the food of loneliness and meditation
He defines his moral obligation his philosophy
   and honor
By means of
He lives in terms of existence

Thus
Uncloche and again
A poet is a meager existence materially

Put clothes on and again
A poet is intellect of possession.

이제야 알았다

세상의 모든 것들
그냥 그렇게 있는 줄만 알았다

한 톨의 씨앗
한 줄기의 실뿌리가
그리도 소중할 줄이야

산전수전 고난의 세월 겪고 나니
귀하고 소중하지 않는 것
하나도 없음을 이제야 알았다

죽어가는 씨앗의 아픔도
척박한 땅 속에 묻혀 생명수를 퍼 올리기 위한
저 처참한 실뿌리들의 몸부림치는 모습도

어버이의
한(恨) 많은 청춘이 피눈물 나는 아픔인줄
이제야 알았다

Now I Understand

Now I understand
All the things in the world
Exist in that way

One seed
Very thin roots of a stem
Are very important

I suffered unspeakable hardships
Now I became aware of
That there are nothing
Precious and valuable

The pain of a dying seed
The thin roots writhe in agony
To absorb subterranean water

Now I understand
The regrettable grief of
Shedding bitter tears
In the young days of parents.

은하의 별밤

우주를 이룬 공간엔
안개꽃으로 피어난 별 밭이 있다
크고도 작은
깊고도 넓은 빛의 여운 따라
저마다의 이름을 갖고
생멸(生滅)의 길을 걷고 있다

저 별은 네 것
이 별은 내 것
주인 없는 별까지도
삶의 가치를 지니고 반짝이는 밤의 공간들

오늘은 주연(主演)이 되어 빛나다
내일은 조연(助演)이 되어 사그라지는
신비의 안개꽃다발

시공의 세계에는
언제나 용기와 희망만이 반짝이는
청정한 별밭의 축제다

Night Stars in the Milky Way

In the space that consists of the cosmos
There is a star field of fog flowers
The stars are big or small
According to the resonance of
Deep and wide light
Each star has its name
Walk along the way of birth and death

That star is yours
This star is mine
Even the star that has not a host
Has the value of living
Twinkles in the night spaces

Today the star as a leading actor twinkles
Tomorrow the star as a supporting actor recedes
It is a mysterious bunch of fog flowers

In the world of time and space
Always only courage and hope glitter
It is the pure and undefiled feast of star field.

두려운 신혼(新婚)

누가 누구인지
얼굴도 모르고
점지된 삶이란 뜻에 따라
한 생을 살았건만

세월 좋아
젊음은 자유이듯
재 뜻 따라 살아가는 인생들

짝은 있되 둥지가 없어
짝짓기는 싫다지만
까치둥지
제비집에
철따라 옮겨 살다보면

베란다에 지은 50평 아지트엔
삼대(三代)가 지지배배
행복이 까악까악 물들어질 텐데

The Fearful Honeymoon

Who is who
Without knowing faces each other
According to the fortunate blessing
Although we have lived a whole life

The time trend of life is good
As youth is freedom
The couple live a whole life at their pleasure

There is mate but here is no nest
Although they dislike mating
The nests of Korean magpies
The nests of swallows
Move by seasons

A hiding place of 50 pyong
That was built in the verandah
Three generations would live happily 'jijibebe'
Happiness would be 'gaak-gaak'

커피 잔에 담긴 추억

커피향이 필적마다
그리워지는 당신

그 속에 묻혀 스며든
당신의 하얀 미소
따뜻하고 인자하신 그 모습
영원히 지울 수 없는 추억입니다

한 모금에 "맛있다, 맛있어"
또 한 모금에 이렇게 맛있을 수가를 연발하시며
"어쩜
네 사랑은 이렇게도 향기롭고 진하단 말이냐" 하시던
나의 신
나의 아버님

오늘도 따끈한 커피 잔을 마주하면
추억어린 당신의 발자국을 뒤척이며
한 모금
또 한 모금을 음미해 봅니다

Remembrance in a Cup of Coffee

I yearn you Dear Father
Whenever the aroma of coffee emits

White smile and benignant shape in it
Unforgettable and eternal remembrance

A bit of coffee flavorous
Another bit of coffee flavorous
What shall I do?
Father said "Dear son your love
Is so much abundant like coffee"
You are my Father like Almighty God

Even today before a cup of hot coffee
I taste each bit of coffee thinking of Father.

가깝고도 먼 길

존재의 존재가
함께이고 따로 인데
어찌 가깝고도 멀다하지 않겠나

마주보는 연습
손잡는 연습
열심히 하다보면 닿아있는 곳 어디이며

마음 따로 몸 따로
눈마저 멀어지면
어디 서있는 인생이 될까

Near and Distant Way

Existence of existence
Together with and separate
Why would you not say that
It is near and distant?

Drill of seeing face to face
Drill of gripping hands
If I do something earnestly
I would know the place where I am

Separate spirit and separate body
If also eyesight becomes poor
Where does the life stand?

삶

삶이란 돌고 도는 원(圓)의 세계다
때로는 궤도를 이탈하여
수평선을 그리기도 하고
수직의 묘기를 부리다가
추락의 맛을 감내하는 것

삶이 그렇게 늪에 빠질지라도
슬픔이나 자책은 금물이며
인내(忍耐)의 미덕(美德)이 깊어질수록
궤도를 찾아 원으로 돌아가리니

현재는 욕심과 허영의
미완의 결정체며
미래는 언제나 꿈과 희망의 메시지만 생성되리니

Living

Living itself is a circle of turning round
Sometimes living secedes the orbit
It draws a horizon
Doing a miraculous feat or verticality
To go through an accidental fall

Although living falls into a marsh
Sorrow and self-reproach prohibit
Deeper perseverance and virtue
Living seeks the orbit and
Returns to the original circle

Present is a unfinished crystal
Of avarice and vainglory
Future always consists of
The message of dream and hope.

겨울 강변에
— 미련

마음이 음산해지는 날
보고픔이 그리움 되어 노를 저어간다

떠나고 없는 너를
아직도 보내지 못한 이 마음

어쩜 다시는 없을 것 같은 만남
만나야 할 때 헤어지고
헤어져야 할 때 사랑하고픈 마음인데

네가 떠난 자리엔 꽃이 지고 해가 진다

사는 날까지 기다리며
아니, 죽는 날까지 그런 날이 오길

어스름 해가 지고
싸늘함이 엄습해온 겨울 강엔
성긴 눈발이 내려앉아 적요로만 서성인다

At the Winter Riverside

The day when my heart dismal
I oar my way
To see you becomes longing

Even though you are not here now
My heart still has not parted you

I am at a loss we might not meet again
When we should meet we part
When we should part I love you

At the place you departed
Flowers wither and the sun sets

The day would come
I wish to wait until I live

The sun sank at dusk
On the cold winter river
Sparse snow falls
Only silence lingers.

별꽃

지상에 널브러진 꽃눈과
밤하늘에 펼쳐진 별꽃은
전생에 형제였나 보다

모양과 빛과 색감이 그렇고
느낌과 낭만과 추억이 그렇고
설레임과 방황과 사랑 또한 그렇다

화사한 봄밤
황홀한 가슴을 일렁이게 하는
별들의 잔치
꽃눈 내리는 계절이다

Star Flowers

Snow flowers spread out on the ground
Star flowers spread out in the night sky
It seems that they were brothers
In the previous life

The shapes of light and colors are so
Feeling romance and retrospect are so
Also palpitation wandering and love are the same

At the luxurious spring night
The feasts of stars
Sway my ecstatic heart
It is the season of snow flower falling.

고백(1)
— 깨우침의 소리

머나먼 이방(異邦)의 노을을 안고
인생무상의 허물을 벗는다

자존과 오만의 가면 속에
분장된 노을을 쓰고
주연(主演)만을 자처한
나만의 나르시스의 삶

저 드넓은 이국땅의 노을을 보며
초자연의 위상 앞에 서있는
초라한 내 모습이
얼마나 가증스러운 탈을 쓰고 살았는지
솔로몬의 탄식에 호흡이 멎는다

Confession(1)
— The Sound of Awareness

With the twilight of faraway foreign land
Peel off the cuticle of the frailty of human life

In the mask of self-esteem and arrogance
I play the leading part
It is only my life of narcissism

Seeing the twilight of wide foreign land
Before the solemnity of supernaturalism
My shabby figure
How has it been wearing?
A detestable mask
I breathe hard
Due to the lamentation of Solomon.

눈높이만큼의 세상

키 만큼의 높이에서
위만 보고 살아오다
프리즘을 매단 기둥을
하늘 끝에 세워 두고

세콰이어 나무에 집을 짓고 사는
새들에 눈을 맞추니
세상은 온통 하찮은 것들 뿐

나무가 허공을 향해 자라고
새들이 하늘을 향해 높이 날으는 이유를
이제야 알 것 같아

허공에 눈을 맞춰 수평을 이루니
그 곳 또한 더 높고 더 넓은
또 다른 세계가 있음을 알았다

The World of Eye Height

I have lived at the level of eye height
Set a pile of prism in the air

I catch my eyes to the birds
That are living in the cage
On sequoia trees
All the world is full of trivial matters

Trees grow to the air
Now I might know the reason
Why do birds fly hight in the sky?

My eyesight keeps level in the sky
I know that there is a different world
The world is higher and wider.

그리워지는 사람

인연이란 관계 속에
나는 보여주지 않고
상대만 먼저 알려고 하는 세상에
나를 먼저 드러내 놓고
상대의 선택을 선별하는 습관이 있다

이는 거짓과 위선의 탈을 경계하며
순수와 진실과 정의만을 위한 선택의 삶 이었다

이렇게 모난 삶에도
가는 사람 보다 오는 사람이 많았으나
정녕 보내고 싶지 않은 사람 붙잡지 못해
그리워지는 사람이 있다

그 그리움에 지친 허전함과
충혈된 마음으로
기다림과 그리움의 끝자락을 부여잡고
목을 맨다면

가는 자도 보내는 자도
그리움으로 그리워질까

The Yearning People

In terms of affinity
Without any introduction of oneself
Most people wish to know
The other party in advance
But habitually introduce myself first
So that the other party select

Since there is false and hypocritic mask
Precautions ought to be taken
My life style is based upon
Only purity truth and justice

In spite of such particular living
Coming people were more than going people
Because I could not catch
My favorite people who left
I really yearn those people

I am tired with yearning and feel empty
Thirstily I hold the ends of waiting and yearning
With all my heart

Both going people and sending people
Do they yearn due to yearning?

꿈의 나라

갖고자 하고 얻고자하는
바램을 이루고자
그곳을 찾아 떠나고픈
나만의 길

어디 간들 그런 곳이 없겠느냐마는
태생의 뿌리를 찾아
바람과 햇살이 잘 드는
꿈의 숲길 찾아 나선다

많고도 많은 그 좋은 곳 다 버리고
하늘의 말씀이 깃들고
내 마음 편히 쉬어 잠들 수 있는
나만의 은밀한 공간
꿈의 나라로

The Land of Dream

To have or to earn
To achieve the wishes
I desire to search for the place
It is only my way

Wherever such places would be
In search for the root of
The breeze and sunny path
The forest of dream

Abandon a lot of nice places
Where God's sayings are
And with my whole heart would sleep
It should be only my covert place
To the land of dream.

삶이란 돌고 도는 원(圓)의 세계다
때로는 궤도를 이탈하여
수평선을 그리기도 하고
수직의 묘기를 부리다가
추락의 맛을 감내하는 것

Living itself is a circle of turning round
Sometimes living secedes the orbit
It draws a horizon
Doing a miraculous feat or verticality
To go through an accidental fall

제2부

그대의 모습

Your Shape

그대여

그대여
이렇게 호젓한 날
그리움이 있다는 건
얼마나 아름다운 일인가

그리움과 보고픔을 넘어
사랑에 취하고 싶은
그대가 있다는 건
얼마나 경이로운 일인가

멀리서 가까이서
그대가 내 안에 있음이
얼마나 행복한 일이며
내가 존재하는 기쁨이 아닌가

그대여
이 기쁨 이 행복 있기에
우리들의 붉게 타는 노을길이
더욱 더 아름답지 않은가

Dear Darling

Dear Darling
It is very quiet today
How much is it beautiful!
That there is yearning

Beyond yearning and seeing
I am intoxicated with love
It is amazing that
You are near me

Distantly or near
That you are in my heart
Is greatly happy
Also it is the pleasure of existence

Dear Darling
Owing to the pleasure and happiness
The way of our burning red twilight
Is more beautiful than anything.

회개

아름다움의 절정에
인생의 꽃 피우고 져
내게 온 당신

열정과 보람으로
후회 없는 삶이라 했건만

어느덧 청춘의 꿈은 사라지고
삶이란 허공에 발을 딛고
순수를 가장한 고난의 시간들 뿐

오늘따라
병마에 지쳐 잠든 아내의 모습에
참회의 꽃 피우고저
그의 손톱에 봄을 새겨 넣어준다

Repentance

At the zenith of beauty
You came to me
To bloom the flower of life

With passion and benefit
Though living was without repentance

The dream of youth disappeared
The foot step of living is on the vainness
Time and tide of hardship
That disguises genuineness

Today to the sleeping shape sick wife
In order to bloom the flower of repentance
I put the spring under her nails.

아내의 그림자

초롱초롱한 두 눈동자
레이저로 쏟아지는 눈빛에
말 대신 가슴으로 감싸않은
의지와 절개의 사임당 이었지

다소곳함과 따스한 미소가
유난히도 반짝였던
하늘의 천사란 칭송들

오늘도 수많은 인맥들은
당신의 그 모습 그대로를
가슴에 새겨놓고
잊지 못 할 추억으로 그리워하는구려

The Shadow of Beloved Wife in the Heaven

Your limpid eyes
The expression of your eyes like laser beam
You used to embrace instead of words
You were a Saimdang
Who has volition and integrity

Obedient and warm smile oddly glitters
You are the one of angels
That brighten the stars in the sky

Even today many people
Have the recollection at heart
They yearn that is unforgettable recollection.

그대의 모습

자나 깨나
내 곁에 숨 쉬고 있는 당신
그 모습 그대로 인데
이리도 허전한 마음 왜 일까요

그처럼 반짝이는 눈만 깜박이며
내게 주는 무언(無言)의 속삭임들
알듯 모를 듯 고개를 끄덕였지만
진정 당신의 마음 읽을 수 없었음에
가슴에 멍이 들었다오

마지막 단 한 마디라도
알아들을 수 있었더라면
이렇게 외롭고 허전하진 않았을 텐데

Your Shape

When I am asleep or awake
You breathe beside me
Your shape as it is
Why do I feel so empty

Twinkling eyes blink
You give me wordless whisper
Although I nodded as if I know
Because I couldn't understand your thinking
It is heartbreaking to me

It I could hear the last me word
I would not so much lonely and empty.

그립다 아니 그리워

그립다 아니 그리워
그리워 말라
청산에 푸르른 백엽이 질 때 까지
살고 죽자던 굳은 맹세의 언약

허약함에 눌려 베인 자국에
봇물 터지듯 무너져 내린
가녀린 님이여

그리도 무심히 떠나버리면
한(恨) 많은 그 아픈 상처
어이 하라고
오늘도 먼 산만 바라보며
한숨만 짓는 구려

삶이 그런 건지
세월이 그런 건지
말벗도 의지할 곳도 없음에
외로움만 지척이네요

Yearn and Yearn

Yearn and yearn
Do not yearn
Until the green leaves fall in the mountain
The promise of believable pledge of
Altogether live and die

A cut scratch of frailty
Like busted up irrigation water
Week Dear love

You departed very detachedly
Dew to a deplorable scratch
What shall I do?
Even today I sigh looking at
The distant mountain

Is living or time like that
Neither a companion to chat with
Nor a supporter
Only solitude surrounds me.

비오는 날의 소고(小考)

여보!
비가 오네

장독대며 빨래는 어떻게 하지
소리치자

면사포를 쓰듯 고개 숙인 꽃들이
얄밉다는 듯 쳐다보고 있다

이걸 어쩌나
당신이 그토록 좋아하던
수선화며 튤립이며
화려한 장미꽃 동산을

내 무능과 무심의 관능에
자책과 자학을 하고 있을 때

하늘을 가르는 광란의 빛줄기가
폭우를 쏟고 있다

여보! 미안해
이걸, 어떻게 하지

Thinking of a Rainy Day

Hello Honey
Now it is raining

I shout at the earthenware pot
Of soy sauce in the terrace
And the place for drying clothing

Flowers which lower their heads
As if wear wedding veils
Look upward detestably

What shall I do?
You like so much the flower garden
Of daffodils tulips and roses

When I reproach and torment myself
Against my inefficiency and inadvertence

Rain falls down furiously
As if a heavy rainfall Would cut the sky

Hello Honey I am sorry
What shall I do?

이 가을에 갖고 싶은 사람

고즈넉한 가을향기에 어울리는
풋풋한 사랑 하나 갖고 싶다

감성(感性)과 지각(知覺)이 깨어있어
느낌과 눈빛만으로도
진실과 행복이 느껴지는
그런 사람 하나 갖고 싶다

화려하지도 향기롭지도 않은
코스모스처럼 은은하게 풍겨오는
갈바람의 향을 타고
내 곁에 와주는
그런 사람 하나 갖고 싶다

지성(知性)과 해안(解顔)이
짜릿한 솔향기처럼 녹아내려
온몸 가득 풍겨오는
그런 사람 하나 품고 싶다

I Hope to meet such Person in Autumn

In this silent fragrant autumn
I wish to have a refreshing sweetheart

She should be emotional and perceptible
By only feeling and the expression of her eyes
I would feel genuineness and happiness
I hope to meet such person in Autumn

Neither luxurious nor fragrant
A faint fragrance of cosmos
Coming to me with autumn wind
I wish to have such person

Intelligence and gentleness melt down
As the piquant fragrance of pine trees
And give forth a scent of whole body
I wish to embrace such person.

꽃눈 내리던 날

차가움을 벗어난 바람이
옷깃을 스칠 때면
어김없이 날아든 꽃눈사랑

동토의 뼈를 깎아
혈(血)을 용해해 내는
그 화려한 무대 속에
상춘객들이 너울너울 꽃 춤을 춘다

허나
내겐 잊을 수 없는 사랑
영혼(靈魂)의 신을 배웅해야 하는
차가운 햇살 이었다

꽃눈이 펑펑 내리던 날
오늘도 그날처럼 존재의 뜰을 찾아
가족과 함께 어버이의 하늘 집에 나들이 간다

Flower Snow Falling Day

When cold wind is awestruck
The love of flower snow always comes

Whittle bones of frozen land
After melt blood
On the luxurious stage of spring
Sightseers dance with swaying arms

However
To me unforgettable love
I should send off the God of soul
It was cold sunlight

The day when flower snow was heavily falling
Today we seek the field of existence
Families pay a visit to the Heaven house of parents.

동백 아가씨

까마득한 어린 시절
청운의 꿈을 안고 한양(漢陽) 길에 올랐건만
대학입학시험 중에 쓰러져 수술을 받고
저승길을 헤매다 돌아오던 날

싸늘한 칼바람에 섞인 눈발은
펄펄 쌓여만 가고
가누진 못한 몸으로
산동네의 계단을 올라야만 했다

한 계단 두 계단 두려움에 떨고 서 있을 때
어디선가 불현 듯 나타난 동백 아가씨
붉은 마후라 걸어주며
춥지 않느냐는 말 한마디
날 일으켜 세워 집 앞까지 올려놓은
용광로 가슴이었다

The Lady of a Camellia Flower

Long time ago when I was young
I had lofty ambitions and
Applied for a university in Seoul
I fell down in the middle of
The entrance examination
Received a medical operation
I wandered the journey of the next world
In the day on the way home

Snow was falling in cold wind
When I could not keep the balance of my body
Going up home on the hill

When I was tremble with fear
Suddenly a lady went past by me
She was a camellia flower lady
Hanged a red muffler on my neck
She said that it is very cold
She took me at the front of my house
Her heart was warm like a blazing furnace

훗날
행여, 행여나 만날 수 있으려나
헤아려 본 세월들
오늘같이 눈이 내리는 날엔
불현 듯 스쳐가는 동백꽃 아가씨

Some time passed since that day
By some chance
I have waited in case she might drop by
Much time and tide has passed
Like today when snow faills
Suddenly I think of the camellia flower lady.

연서(戀書)

가슴에 품은 외마디 하나

꿈길에선 꽃으로 피었다가
붓을 들면 사라지고
가슴은 불타는데
몸은 멀리 있어
중천금(重千金)만한 한마디

또 다시 용기를 내 보지만
백지엔 무지갯빛만 아롱거려
활활 불꽃만 피우는 구려

그대여
어찌 언어로만 표현해야 사랑이나요
벙어리 냉가슴 불꽃으로라도 타오른다면
그것이 아니던가요

A Love Letter

A word in my heart

It blooms on the way of flower
But it disappears
When I grip a pen to write a poem
My heart is burning
Body is at a disdant place
One precious and valuable word

Even though I take my courage
On a sheet of paper once again
The colors of a rainbow dapple
Only it bursts into flames

Dear Darling
Why love should be expressed in words
A dumb person who is in silence
Should flame out
It would be love.

겨울 바다의 초상

북적거리는 화려함 보다
냉정과 싸늘함이 깃든
겨울 바다를 찾는다

을씨년스런 하늘과 바람
그 속을 가르는 눈발의 정취가
모처럼 가슴을 뚫리게 하고

하늘과 바다가 뒤엉켜
지상으로 내려앉는
아슴푸레한 선(線) 하나
세상은 온통 하얀 면사포를 쓴
축제의 장이 펼럭일 뿐

몇날 며칠이 무섭도록
펑펑 내려앉은 자리엔
인적이 끊긴지 이미 오랜 시간
섧도록 경이로운 설경(雪景)에 갇혀
생(生)을 유추하는 시간의 상념(想念)

The Portrait of Winter Sea

I seek the winter sea
Coolness and cold sea
Rather than bustling and luxury

Dreary sky and wind
The mood of snow flakes put across
After a long interval
The mood cuts cleared my heart

Sky and sea get entangled
And get down on the ground
A faint line
The earth wears a white wedding veil
It is in a festival mood

It snowed very much for several days
Long time ago tranquility regained over
Sorrowfully amazing scene of snow confines
And analogizes life
And the meditation of time.

잃어버린 용기
— 연서

영롱한 별 하나
별똥별이 되어 내 곁에 왔다

낯설고 뜨거워 가까이 할 수 없는
허나, 만져보고 소유하고픈
불덩이 하나

사랑도 용기라면
운명 또한 용기랄까

내 가엾은 연서(戀書) 한 장
네 창가를 맴돌다가
그만 싸늘하게 식어버린
별똥별 하나

The Lost Courage

— A Love Letter

A brilliant star
It became a meteor
And fell beside me

I could not approach near by it
Because it was strange and hut
But I touched the burning stone

If love is courage
It should be destiny and courage

My pathetic love letter
It was spinning round the window
A last the meteor has gotten cold.

산사의 길

속세와 다른 길을 걷겠다고
찾아든 산속의 토굴

바깥세상을 안에 들이고자
뜬구름까지 잡아들여
갈증의 염원을 구애하며
묵도(默禱)의 길을 닦고 있다

풍경(風磬)소리 찾아든
세인(世人)들의 발자국들
고요가 흐르는 달빛에 그만
발가벗겨진 초로(草露)의 마음 되어

인내와 풍요를 가득 담고
사랑의 꽃씨 뿌리며
하산(下山)의 그날을 기다림 한다

The Way of a Mountain Temple

To go to the different way of mundane life
Became a cave dweller

To draw outworld into inworld
Drag in floating clouds
Love thirsty wishes trait
Offer a moment of silent prayer

The foot stops of mundane people
Who search for the sound of wind bell
By the silent moonlight
Become the bare and pure dew on the grass

With full perseverance and abundance
Sprinkle flower seeds of love
Wait for the day of
Climbing down of a mountain.

감성(感性)과 지각(知覺)이 깨어있어
느낌과 눈빛만으로도
진실과 행복이 느껴지는
그런 사람 하나 갖고 싶다

She should be emotional and perceptible
By only feeling and the expression of her eyes
I would feel genuineness and happiness
I wish to have such person

제3부

꿈길에서
On the Way of a Dream

꿈길에서
— 사모곡

까아만 밤하늘에
유난히도 반짝이는 별들이 쏟아지네요

그 속엔 하얀 미소로 꽃피어
방글방글 반겨주신 님

섧도록 그리운
그 모습
참으로 오랜만이네요

아버님도 잘 계시지요

언뜻 언뜻
소름 돋도록 피어나는
그 옛날 그 모습들이
주마등으로 비쳐오네요

어머니
그리운 어머니
나의 사랑 나의 신이신
어머니

On the Way of a Dream
— Thinking of Mother

In the dark night sky
Unusually twinkle stars fall down

Among them the flower of white smile
You greet me with a broad smile

Wistfully yearning
Your shape
Really it is a long time

How is your Father?

Unexpectedly
It is gooeseflesh all over
Your shapes of once upon a time
Are brought back as kaleidoscope

Yearning Mother
You are my Mother like Almighty God
Dear Mother I love you!

고백(2)
— 사부곡

야속한 게 세상인가 보네요
피땀 흘려
죽도록 키워왔던 피붙이들이
배신 아닌 배신으로
막가는 인생길을 걷고 있네요

잘 되라 잘 되어야 한다
정화수 받쳐 놓고
성공과 행복위한 고난의 세월 보냈건만
무슨 불만 그리 많아
인륜을 저버리는지

피땀 흘려 키워온 노고(勞苦)가
그리도 못마땅하여
그 업보 그 슬픔 받고 가야 하나요

Confession(2)

— Thinking of Father

It seems that present society is unsympathetic
Offspring have been raised by blood and sweat
They have easily betrayed their parents
Their behavior is rambunctious

You should succeed for all life
Parents used to draw water from
The well at day break and prayed
And had sent time and tide in distress
Of success and happiness of children
What's all that complaints
They might go contrary to morality

The travail of blood and sweat
Is so disagreeable and distasteful
Should I receive retribution for
The deeds of a former life and sorrow.

호반

헤아릴 수 없이 넓은
너무도 깊은 그리움이다

산의 하반신을 끊어 안고
쉴 새 없이 흐르는 정을 껴안고

물속을 날으는 새들의 그림자며
두둥실 떠도는 흰 구름 몇 점

조석(朝夕)으로 변해가는
은파(銀波)를 바라보며
정지된 내 모습에
그리움만 서성거린다

The Shore of a Lake

A lake is countless and wide
It is too deep longing

A lake arms the lower half of a mountain
It arms restlessly flowing affection

The shadow of birds that flies in the water
Few pieces of floating white clouds

I look at silvery waves
That change in the morning and evening
In the motionless shape of mine
Only longing hovers about.

밝은 미래

좋은 환경과 조건
좋은 사람 찾지 말고
내가 먼저 그렇게 되어 봄이 어떨까

예쁘고 착한 아름다움만 탐하지 말고
내 스스로 그런 사람 되어주면 어떨까

새롭고 행복한 삶 추구치 말고
먼저 손 내밀어
그 길 만들어 감이 더 좋지 않을까

사고(思考)가 넓고 깊을수록
찾고 탐하는 것보다
배려와 베풂으로 다가가
그 길을 쌓아감이 행복이 아니려나

The Bright Future

You might not seek
Good environment condition and a good person
In the first place I could be such person

Do not desire prettiness goodness and beauty
How about myself become such person?

Do not pursue new and happy living
Reach out your hand first
It should be better to make such way

The more thinking is wide and deep
Do not seek and desire
Approach solicitude and alms
It would be happy to make such way.

시(詩)

고뇌와 침묵으로 태어나
말과 행동으로 삶을 갖고
철학과 사상으로 진리를 남기는 것

일생을 갈고 닦아
시를 닮고자
흉내를 내보고
처신을 자처해 보지만
아직도 뒤뚱뒤뚱 걸음마에
넘어지기 일쑤다

그러면서도
빛과 소리의 환희가
무언(無言)의 감성으로 가슴을 두드리면
쏟아 붓지 않고는 못 배기는 버릇
즐거움이고 환희이며
괴로움이고 고통의 산물이다

A Poem

A poem is born upon agony and silence
It has lived with words and behaviors
Philosophy and thought result in truth

All my life I have whetted
To resemble a poem
Imitate and pretend to be a good poet
Still unstable steps fall to topple

Nevertheless
Jubilancy of light and sound
Do the heart good with silent sensitivity
I should write poems habitually
It is glee and jubilancy
Poems are products of agony and pain.

시인은

시인은 통할 듯 통하지 않는
함께이면서도 따로 인
이승과 저승의 양 날개를 달고
걷는 듯 날으며
날으는 듯 꿈으로 사라지는
사라지는 듯 영혼의 불사조가 된
신(神)의 존재

A Poet

A poet is comprehended or not
He is together or not
He bears two wings of
This world and the other world
He flies as if he walks
He disappears into a dream
As if he flies
He has become a phoenix of soul
It seems that
The existence of God.

어느 별에서

어두울수록 영롱해지는
멀수록 아련해지는
작을수록 반짝여지는
그런 존재

어느 별에서 왔기에
그토록 그리워지는가

목마른 갈증에 사랑이 돋듯
언제 떠났기에
저토록 차가운 빛으로 서서
눈꽃만 날리는 것이더냐

아직도 우리는
이글거리는 모닥불에서
토닥토닥 불꽃을 피우는데

In a Certain Star

The darker the more brilliant is
The farther the vaguer is
The smaller the twinkler is
Such existence is a paragon

Came from a certain star
Yearning so much

As I quench my thirst for love
When did you depart?
You stand with very cold light
Only did you fly snow flowers

Still
We are from the burning bonfire
We are rapping the flames.

깊은 사랑
— 그는

긴긴 세월
방황의 끝을 잡지 못해
점점 멀어져만 가는 희망의 순간들

묵묵히 바라보며
아는 듯 모르는 듯 내 곁을 맴도는 사람

어느 누구도 사랑을 주지 않을 때
창문을 스쳐 눈길을 주는 이

실의에 빠져 죽음을 고하는 순간에도
은밀한 기도로 용기와 희망을 불어넣어준 사람

모두가 떠나간 빈자리에 홀로 서서
손잡아 일으켜 세워준 그이

아무도 관심 밖인 나를 지켜보며
기다리지도 않은 그 먼 시간동안 사랑을 보내준
아니, 사랑을 고하기 전부터 기다려준 단 한사람

Deep Love

Long long time
Swerve from the right path
The moments of hopes become faraway

You see me silently and
Turn around me

When nobody loves me
You gives me eyesight through windows

Disappointed moment was near death
Silently pray courage and hope for me

All people left you alone
Gripped my hands to stand up

When nobody cared for me
You kept your eyesight on me
During the faraway time
Rather you are the only one person
Before mentioning love
Who has been waited for me.

자화상
— 따르고 싶은 삶

부모님 슬하에서
팔년 만에 태어난 귀하디귀한 자식
잃어버린 조국 되찾았으나
가난과 병마에 시달려
죽음의 고개 넘나들며
간신히 부여잡은 허약한 생명

풍전등화(風前燈火) 같은 생명 살리고자
얼마나 무거운 짐 살으셨을까

그뿐이랴
전쟁으로 생긴 고아들 뒷바라지에
죽음에 이른 양노원의 노파(老派)들 까지
밤낮을 헤아려 보살펴온 삶

참선(參禪)의 길
성인(聖人)의 길
하늘의 뜻이 아니었을까

Self-Portrait

In the eighth year of parental marriage
I was born as an exalted and beloved son
The lost fatherland had been recovered
However under poverty and sickness
Owing to I was taken ill I went and came often
The threshold of life and death
Hardly I has survived as feebly

At that time my life was like
The light before the wind
Parents did the best to save my life
It was really a strenuous effort

It was not all
Parents looked after the orphans
Of the tragic the Korean War
Also the asylum of old people
Parents took care of weak people night and day

The helpful work is
The way of meditation in zen buddhism
The way of religion saints
Also it is a profound meaning of the Heaven

그 거룩한 뜻 이어받고자
한 생을 살았건만
얼마나 받들었을까
보람과 후회의 자책에
뉘우침과 반성의 길만 남는다

During my lifetime I have made
An effort to succeed the divine grace
Because of the self-reproach of worth and
remorse
Only contrition and reflection have remained.

손님
— 방문객

사람 사는 집에
사람이 온다는 건
얼마나 행복한 일인가

그러나 언제부턴가
사람 사는 집에
사람이 온다는 것이
부담이 되고 짜증이 된 시대

자신들만의 공간에
남이란 존재가 싫어
스스로가 갇히고 싶어서일까

핵가족이 된 세상
서로가 더불어 함께하는 삶이
존재이고 가치일진데
사랑이고 행복이란 걸 어찌 헤아릴까!

Guests
— Visitors

To the living house
People come to the house
How much happy is it?

But in these days
People come to the house
It is a burden and vexation

In their own space of the house
Other people are not welcomed
We would be confined ourselves

Now it is the age of nuclear family
The living of all together
Is desirous trend
Of existence and value
How could we understand love and happiness!

사랑의 길

길 위에 길이 있고
길 밑에 길이 있듯이

길의 시작과 끝점에
그리움이, 사랑이 있다

하늘엔 새가
바다엔 파도가
지상엔 형형색색의 꽃들이
바람 따라 피었다 지듯

우리들의 인생이 피고 지는 곳에도
또 다른 사랑이 되살아나
깊고도 넓은 은혜로 살아간다

The Way of Love

As there is a way on a way
As there is a way under a way

There are yearning and love
At the beginning and end of a way

Birds are in the sky
Waves are in the sea
A great variety of flowers on the ground
Bloom and fall by the wind

At the place where our lives end
Another love revives
We live in the deep and wide blessings.

산책길

고요를 묵상하며
고독과 외로움을 짊어지고
비탈진 산책길을 걷는다

바람이 상큼한 미소로 다가와
함께 가자 팔짱을 끼며
송알 송알 거린다

꽃잎 하나 날아와
내 입술을 덮고
아무 말도, 보지도, 듣지도 말라며
손사래를 친다

이 길에선 오직
자신만을 바라보고 들춰보라며
살며시 다가와 윙크를 한다

A Promenade

I am lost in silent contemplation
With solitude and loneliness
I walk along a hilly promenade

Wind approaches me tenderly smiling
Holding my arms and murmurs

A petal flies to me
And covers my lips
It waves its hands tells me that
Neither see nor hear anything

The petal insists that this way is its promenade
And that I should see itself only
It comes near me and winks.

인생길

길을 가다 보면
갈림길이 있기 마련
이쪽 아니면 저쪽
선택의 길에 따라 목적지도 결과도 달라
전전긍긍 두려움이 앞선다

우리들의 인생길 또한 그렇듯
선택과 책임 또한 그러하다

어느 길이건 생각과 노력의 대가만큼
가깝고도 멀기도 할 터인데

한탕주의에 만연된
권력과 처신이 있는가 하면
뜬구름 잡는 복권 같은 세상이 있어
공정(公正)보다는 불합리한 제도에 싸여
옳고 그름이 헷갈리는 세상길도 있어
참으로 아이러니한 삶이다

The Road of Life

When we go along a road
We meet cross road
Either of them goes to
Different destination and result is fear

As the road of our life
Selection and responsibility are the same

Either way is near and far
According to thinking and effort

It is a lamentable fact that
The strange trend and tolerance are widespread
There is power and demeanor
Also there is a world of lottery
To catch the floating clouds
The unreasonable system rather than fair
Righteous and wrong ways are mixed
Indeed life is really ironical.

어머니
그리운 어머니
나의 사랑 나의 신이신
어머니

Yearning Mother
You are my Mother like Almighty God
Dear Mother I love you!

제4부

둥둥 섬에서

Dungdung Isle in Seoul

지하철의 밤

소나기가 장대비로 퍼붓는
깊은 밤
오갈 데 없는 승객이
자리를 차지하고 숙면에 취해 있다

사랑을 잃어서 일까
서울이 그리워서 일까
온종일 흔들리며 코골이를 한다

빼곡히 들어선 사람들은
불빛을 따라
흔들리는 사잇길을 빠져나와
어둠의 길을 안고 떠나는
빗속의 지하철

서울의 밤은
사랑이고 그리움이며
비애이고 고통인
흔들리는 세상이다

The Night Subway

At a deep night
A sudden shower falls down severely
For a passenger there is no place to go
He is sleeping well

Does he lose love?
Or does he yearn city of Seoul?
All the day he snores in the train
And they go out the shaking by pass
The subway in a dark rainy night

The night of Seoul love and longing
Also it is sorrow and agony
It is the shaking world.

둥둥 섬에서
— 반포 나루터에서

오늘도 그날처럼
하염없는 그리움을 안고
바람 부는 강변에 앉아

가슴 스치는 열차소리에
회상의 날개만 펄럭이고 있다

눈발이 날리고 화려한 츄리의 불빛마저
을씨년스런 밤
텅 빈 가슴에 너를 그려본다

샛별로 반짝이는 눈망울
앙증맞은 미소의 화려함이
동그랗게 동그랗게 물결 타고 흘러간다

나루터의 불빛이 광란의 춤을 추듯
긴 꼬리를 물고 달리는 전철의 빛
또한 광기를 부리는데

Dungdung Isle in Seoul
— The Wings of Reminiscence

Today like the other day
I hold on my arms abstracted yearning
Sit are a windy riverside

At the heartbreaking sound of a train
The wings of reminiscence flutter about

At a dismal night snowflakes fall
The light of the light of
Luxurious ornamental trees is also frenzy
I remind you of the happy days
That we had spent together

Your eyes are like twinkling morning stars
The luxuriously pretty smiles
Are flowing down roundly

The light of a ferry dances in a frenzy
The light running one after another subway
Also flies into a fury

이제 가야지
오지 않을 너를 위해
언젠가는 저 물결처럼 만나야 할
우리들의 그날을 위해

Now I must go for you who doesn’t come
For the our day whenever we meet
For the sake of ourselves
As the waves of water sometime.

운명이란 이름

무성한 바람 소리에
나목을 흔들어 깨우는
님이 온다

푸르른 청춘
절정의 계절에도
열리지 않던 인연(因緣)들

갈색 물들고 서야 알아차린
매서운 깨달음
지친 몸 일으켜 세워 빈자리 내어준다

강 건너
소리 없이 스며든
운명이란 이름

The Word of Fate

The sound of a blast of wind
My beloved who shakes and awakes
Naked trees is coming

The blue youth
At the acme of seasons
Affinities that were not opened

The fierce awareness
After affinities have been dyed brown
Erect tired body
And concede empty seats

Across the river
A word appeared silently
The word is fate.

넝마주이 인생

새벽을 깨워 서두른 자
하루의 행복이 있다기에

굽은 허리 뒤틀린 다리를 끌며
상가며 골목길 돌아
베이고 찔리며 구겨진 생을 한가득 주어 담고
들어선 고물상

수고했다는 말과 함께 건너 받은
천 원짜리 세 장
구겨진 지폐를 펴며
행복담긴 지긋한 미소

허나
한 끼의 목 추김도 안 되는
까마득한 삶
쪽방집 주인의 앙칼진 눈빛을 피해야 하는
저, 잠 못 이루는 삶

The Life of a Ragpicker

A ragpicker rises early and hastes
In pursuit of happiness of the day

His waist is bent
Dragging his feet he turns around
A shopping district and a side street
Cut pricked crumpled his life
Picked used items are full in a rearcar

The dealer in second hand articles
The dealer gave him paper money 3,000 won
The ragpicker spread the crumpled money
And he smiles happily

However it just cheated hunger for a while
Living traces back a vague poverty
He must avert the aggresive eyes of
The owner of wicket room
It would be a sleepless night.

겨울 강에서

바람이 엄습한 겨울 강에는
인적이 끊기고
철새들만 유유자적
갈대밭을 서성인다

강 언덕엔 눈보라가 몰아치고
강물에는 원앙이 춤을 추는데
강바람은 깃을 세워 사랑을 읊고 있다

하루의 정적(靜寂)이 피어나는 순간
사랑의 미로에서 헤매는 그리움 하나
허허롭게 맴돌고만 있다

At the Beside of Winter River

At the besides of winter river
Wind makes a sudden attack
Only migratory birds live comfortably
In the fields of reeds

On the riverside hill snow storm rushed
In the river mandarin ducks dance
River wind pulls up collars and chants love

At the time of tranquility in a day
A yearning wanders about
In the labyrinth of love
It turns round vainly.

길(道)
— 도를 닦는

속세와 다른 모습으로 살겠다는
산새들의 노래 소리

안이 바깥이고
바깥이 곧 안이듯
바라는 갈증 채우고자 목청을 두드린다

울림으로 번진 여운(餘韻)이
빛이 되고 녹음(綠陰)이 되어
산사(山寺)를 수놓고
여유의 사색을 즐기는 노승(老僧)처럼
날개 빛도 고고하다

Cultivate a Religious Mind
— The Path of Morality

The song sound of mountain birds
It is allusion which means by
The intention of different from mundane life

As an inside is an outside
Raise my voice to quench my thirst

The reverberation of echoic sound
Becomes light and the shades of trees
Embroiders a mountain temple meditates
As an aged priest who placidly
The light of wings is proud in loneliness.

폭포 앞에서

떨어지는 폭포수에 몸을 던져
사랑도 슬픔도
그리움도 함께
산산조각 깨어지고 부서져도 좋다

끝끝내 흐르지 않겠다
몸부림치는 것 보다
내가 가야할 때와 놓아야할 때가
언제인가를 느끼는 순간

미련도 추억도 그리움마저 던져
한줌 안개비로 사라질지라도 좋다
하나뿐인 인생길
죽음보다 더 짙은 사랑 하나 있었기에

Before a Fall

I throw myself into a waterfall
All together love sorrow and yearning
They are smashed to pieces
It does not matter at all

I will not flow to the last
Rather than squirming a violent struggle
At the moment I feel when I disappear

Throw all together asininity memory and yearning
I don't mind leaving this world
Only one way of leaving
Because there has been
More passionate love than death.

벗이여

벗이여
이제 우리 부를 때
꽃이여 나비여 새로 부르자

한 많은 세상
피눈물로 일으켜 세워
자유롭게 살았건만
철부지 세대들 까막눈에
옛 길로만 돌아가려하니

벗이여
이제 우리들
그 무지한 세상 벗어나서

꽃으로 나비로 새가 되어
자유롭게 날자구나

Dear Friend

Dear friend
Henceforth
When we call each other
Let us call a flower a butterfly and a bird

In the deplorable world
Established by tears of blood
Though lived freely
The thoughtless generation
The ignorant young people
Try to return to the old way

Dear Friend
Now we get out of the ignorant world

Let us become a flower a butterfly and a bird
Let us fly freely.

살아가는 모습

혼자 가는 길엔
고독과 사색이 있고
둘이 가는 길엔
믿음과 배려와 사랑이 있지만
함께 가는 길에는
우정과 신뢰와 베풂이 존재하듯
더불어 살아가는 연습 하다보면
행복은 덤으로 부풀려지는 낙원인 것을

The Phase of Living

On the way one person goes
There are solitude and meditation
On the way two persons go
Although there are belief solicitude and love
On the way many people go together
As friendship belief and mercy exist
In the course of exercise for living together
Happiness is a paradise of an additional premium.

영성(靈聖)의 기도

하늘의 뜻에 따라
발가벗은 몸으로 이승에 왔다
호의호식(好衣好食) 도취되어
이름 세자 남기고 빈 몸으로 귀천함을
축복과 안식(安息)의 삶에 감사토록 하소서

한 생의 숱한 인연과
잊을 수 없는 소중한 추억들의 희로애락을
슬픔으로 지워지지 않게 하소서

내 삶의 뉘우침과 깨달음에
인색치 않게 꾸짖어 주시고
사랑하는 나의 가족과 친지(親知)들이
슬픔과 외로움을 잊고 살아갈 수 있는
삶의 지혜와 용기를 주소서

The Prayer of Divinity

Owing to the purport of the Heaven
I was born bare in this world
I am intoxicated with
Dressing well and faring richly
I should leave my name in this world
And return to the Heaven
Let me be thankful for
The life of blessing and repose

Lifelong many affinities
And joy anger sorrow and pleasure
Which are unforgettable and precious memories
Should never be erased by means of sorrow

Regret and awareness of my life
Severely scold and rebuke
My loving families and acquaintances
In order that they live without sorrow and
  solitude
Present them with wisdom and courage

이 아름다운 세상
즐겁고 행복하였노라 기억하게 하시고
사랑하는 가족들과 만찬 후 꿈꾸듯
잠 속에서 아름답게 이별토록 하소서

In this beautiful world
Let me remember that
I have lived delightfully and happily
After the last dinner
All together my dear families
Let me beautifully part from this world
In sleeping and dreamy.

무능과 무지의 삶
— 혼자라는 것

내가 나를 지키는 일
내가 나를 다스리는 일
그걸 못하랴 생각하며

의지(意志) 하나 세워 고집 하나 틀어잡고
살면 되는 줄만 알았는데
그게 그리 어려울 줄이야

가방끈이 길고 짧고
부와 명예가 있고 없고 가 아니라
고독과 외로움
대화가 없는 오지의 세상
그것 보다 더한 괴로움 있을까

삶이 뭔지 사랑이 뭔지
인생이 뭔지 모를 때는
당연하다 했건만
그것들을 읽혀 깨달으니
그 보다 더 소중한 자산이 없음을
이제 알았더라

The Life of Incompetency and Ignorance
— To Be Lone

The work that I keep myself
The work that I govern myself
I think that the works are easy

I keep volition and obstinacy
I think that they are enough to live
But I regard it as difficulty

The length of schooling
Wealth and honor of parents
They do not much matter
Solitude and loneliness
The life in a hinter land
Without conversation
That are no more afflicting works

When I did not know
What living love and life are
I take as a matter of course
Now I am convinced of my mistake
And now I appreciate that there are
No more precious assets

삶이란 그렇게 어리석고 무능한 것인가
아님, 나 자신의 무능이
그토록 어리석었단 말인가

Living might be stupid and incompetent
Or I am so stupid and in competent myself.

멋진 노년의 품격

얼굴엔 밝은 미소
마음에는 여유로움
몸에는 한결같은 품격을
가슴엔 사랑으로 가득 채워
충만한 삶을 향유하며
과거도 미래도 다 벗어놓고
오늘만을 즐기려는 자

유머와 활력으로 세련미를 갖추고
마음편한 호감으로
뭇 시선을 끌어안는
대인의 자질이
멋진 노년의 품격이 아닐까

The Grace of Fascinating Old Age

Bright smile on the face
Leisure in the mind
Constant grace in the body
Full love in the heart
Possesses replete life
Throws off past and future
He enjoys only today

He prepared completely refined beauty
With humore and vitality
Affords favorable impression
Draws closer all the eyesights of others
The natural gift of an adult of virtue
That is the grace of fascinating old age.

아름다운 노년(老年)

노년이란 늙음이 아니라
지혜와 여유로움의 대명사다

삶의 여정에 명예와 권력과 금력을 버리니
시기와 질투가 떠난 그 자리에
사랑과 너그러움만 존재하여

원망 보다 감사를
미움 보다 축복을
욕심 보다 베풂이 더해져
여유롭고 자유로워지는 것

남는 게 오직 시간뿐이어
쉬엄쉬엄 구름도 주위도 쳐다보며
빈 마음의 여백을 정(情)으로 가득 채우니
사랑이 넘쳐 풍요롭고 고귀함이 아름다워
멋과 존경스러움으로 울어나지 않는가

Beautiful Old Age

Old age is not being old
But is a pronoun of wisdom and leisure

In the journey of life
Discard honor power and money
In the place where jealousy and envy left
Love and generosity remain

Gratitude rather than reproach
Blessing rather than hatred
Mercy rather than greed
And becomes leisurely and free

Gradually look up clouds
And look around surroundings
Feelings are filled in empty heart
Overflowing love is abundant
Noble and beautiful
Dandyism and respect overflow.

샛별로 반짝이는 눈망울
앙증맞은 미소의 화려함이
동그랗게 동그랗게 물결 타고 흘러간다

Your eyes are like twinkling morning stars
The luxuriously pretty smiles
Are flowing down roundly

제5부

바다의 초상
The Portrait of Sea

독립문 공원
— 바람의 눈물

서대문엔
역사의 증인이 세기를 넘어
두 눈을 부릅뜨고 서 있다

인간의 피를 먹고 자란
사람들의 아들이 된 미루나무
역사의 뒤안길에서
그 처참한 삶을 향해 부르짖었던
대한독립만세
태극기의 함성들

오늘도 가슴앓이 눈물을 흘리며
바람으로 흔들리고 있다
바람소리로 한(恨)을 풀고 있다

The Park of Independence
— Tear of Wind

At the old site of Seodaemun Prison in Seoul
Over a century a witness stands
With the angry look in the eyes

Poplar trees which grew from blood of
　humanbeings
Standing at the back street of history
To the miserable people
They roars with rage a furrah
Independence of Korea
Taegeuki The National Flag of Korea
It was a great outcry

Even today people shed tears of remorse
That is heartrending tears
The sounds of winds
Bear a bitter grudge.

바다의 초상

바다는 말이 없고
손도 발도 아무것도 없다

오직
밀려왔다 밀려가는 소리의 여운
가슴 치는 파도만 있을 뿐

그 속엔
사랑과 그리움의 여운이 있고
기쁨과 슬픔의 미련도 있어

천년을 넘나들며
가슴을 두드리는 천의 소리가 있다

The Portrait of Sea

Sea is wordless
And limbless
There is nothing at all

Only reverberations of ebb and flow
And heartbreaking wavers

In the sea
There a resonance of love and yearning
Also there are delight sorrow
And lingering attachment

Going and coming on thousand
There are one thousand sounds of heart
throbbing.

미완의 존재

교양과 상식은 말에서 나오고
학문과 지식은 행동에서 나오며
철학과 사상은
뜨거운 열정과 가슴에서 폭발하는 것

인간은 누구나
자신의 눈높이에서
보고 듣고 생각하며 행동하지만

독선과 아집에 사로잡혀
현실과 변화를 부정하고픈
어리석은 생각들

하여,
인생은 미완성의 존재라는 것

Unfinished Existence

Refinement and commonsense come from speech
Scholarship and knowledge come from behavior
Philosophy and thought explode
In the ardent passion and heart

Though anybody sees listens thinks
And conducts by eye measurement

By means of complacence and egocentricity
Denies reality and variations
It is a foolish decision

At any rate
A human being is unfinished existence.

인간의 속성

우연한 만남에도
그리워지는 사람이 있고

필연적인 만남에도
잊혀지는 사람이 있다

필요할 때 찾아오는 사람이 있고
필요할 때 내 곁을 떠난 사람도 있다

인간이란
우연히 인연되고
인연에 공들이면 필연이 되듯

생을 바쳐
그리워지는 사람
잊혀지지 않는 사람이 되었으면

The Attribute of Humanbeing

To an accidental encounter
There us a longing person

To an inevitable encounter
There is a forgetful person

There is a person who domes
At necessary time
There is a person who leaves
At necessary time

Humanbeing
As accidental becomes affinity
Elaborate affinity becomes inevitability

I wish that I would be
A lifelong yearning and unforgettable person.

작은 가슴 큰 사랑

아침 마다
띵동
작은 사랑이 온다

꼬막 같은 작은 손엔
올망졸망

정(情)도
마음(心)도
사랑(愛)도
가득 가득 들려있다

목발 짚는 친구의
멍에를 지고
오손도손 나누는
큰 빛 사랑이여

작은 가슴
큰 사랑
영원하여라

Little Heart and Great Love

Every morning
Ding-dong
Little love come

Small hands holds ark shell porridge
In a lovely ruddle

Sentiment
Heart
Love
All are fully carries about

A friend walks on crutches
Put the yoke of love or oneself
Talks intimately
Love of great light

Little heart
Great love
Be eternal.

갈대의 꿈

삶의 고뇌를
햇볕에 그을리며
강바람 따라
하늘하늘
솜꽃을 피우던 날

곧은 허리
나부끼며
세파에 휩쓸려도
꿈을 낳은
하얀 꽃
노을을 타고
청조 빛 하늘아래
꿈을 띄워라

The Dream of a Reed

The anguish of living sunburns
Along the wind a river
Cotton flowers are in full glory

Straight waist flutters
It is tossed about by
The angry waves of wind
The white flowers bear a dream
A the sunset
Under the blue sky
Fly a dream.

강강술래

동천에 떠오른 휘영청 밝은 달
구슬땀으로 피어난 오곡백과는
만삭된 몸으로 금빛 물결 일렁이고
서편의 아낙네들 색동옷 팔랑이며
손발 맞춰 돌고 도는 굴렁쇠처럼
굴래 굴래 강강술래 발걸음도 가볍다
개수나무 방아 찧는
그늘 밑에서 푸르게 영글어간
원시림의 사랑

Ganggang Sulae

In the east sky the moon beams down
All kinds of grains of beads of sweat
Golden wave of parturiency
The womenfolk of west flutter
Rainbow striped garments
Like a trundle noop
Gulae gulae, ganggang sulae
Steps are soft
Under the green shade
Love of a primeval forest
The treadmill of a cinnamon tree.

은반위의 요정

유리빛 쟁반위에
춤추는 요정
차이코프스키 음률 속에
은구슬 구르듯
화려한 나비는
형상을 그린다

학(鶴)처럼 우아한
나래 펴든 요정은
미끄러진 칼날위에
또르르 구르며
그렇게 찬란한
빛을 가꾼다

바람처럼 새처럼
날렵한 율동이
무지갯빛 수를 놓아
꽃을 피우듯
저렇게 빛을 가꾼
또 하나의 신비여

The Fair on a Silver Tray

A dancing fairy
On a glass light tray
In the melody of Tchaikovsky
As a silver bead rolls over
The gorgeous butterfly
Draw a shape

The fairy spreads her wings
She is elegant as a red crowned crane
And slides the blade of the skate
Shines so lustrous light

Like winds and birds
Daintily rhythmic movement
Embroiders the colors of rainbow
It is blooming and shining
The genius of the fairy reveals anther mystery.

행복 가꾸소서

해 맑은 하늘 아래
봉우리져 탐스럽게 피어나는 장밋빛 향과
오색찬란한 가을 햇살의 풍성함이
자연의 극치라면

잃어버린 꿈의 조각 찾아
헤매며 기다린 반평생의 시간 속에
사랑의 진주빛 옥구슬이
재 짝을 찾았으니
이보다 더 큰 아름다움이
어디 있을고

그대들
무서리 내린 백발에도
잊지 못한 그리움 찾았으니
행복의 단꿈 애드벌룬 띄우고
깊은 사랑의 맛 흠뻑 마시어
청춘을 즐겁게
인생을 보람되게
한 많은 꿈을 가꾸소서

The Pursuit of Happiness

Under the clear sky
The fragrance of very beautiful roses
The bun dance of shining brilliant
Autumn sunlight is the zenith of nature

Seeking the pieces of lost dream
In the wondering the half of my life
The pearled jew it of love found pair
There no more beautiful than this

Though your hairs are gray
You have sought unforgettable longing
Fly an ad balloon of a happy dream
Inhale the taste of deep love
Enjoy youth and be worth while living
Raises grudging dream
Love give birth love
Happiness gets pregnant with happiness

사랑은 사랑을 낳고
행복은 행복을 잉태하나니

뒤늦은 만남이라 후회지 말고
씨 뿌려 가꾸어
탐스런 열매로 인생을 노래하소서

아름다움은 가꾸는 자의 것이며
행복은 스스로 쌓아가는 결실이리니

그대들
늦음을 새로움으로 승화시켜
밝고 맑은 탐스런 꽃으로 활짝 피어

행복이 이것이었음
말하게 하소서
인생의 꽃이 이렇게 아름답다는 것을
느끼게 하소서

Don't regret a late encounter
Seed and grow a desirable fruit
And sing a happy life

Beauty belongs to grower
Happiness makes the fruit by itself

Lateness assimilates newness
Blooms a clear and beautiful flower

Let me say that happiness is so
Let me feel that the flower of life
Is so beautiful.

자랑스런 나의 형제여

황금물결 나부끼는 광장에
찬란한 그대들의 영광
성총의 빛으로 눈부시구나

남도의 벌판 태봉산 자락에 둥지를 튼지
어언 40여 성상
형제들의 불타는 가슴
뜨거운 열정이
오늘의 역사 이루었으니
감격의 날이요, 영광의 축복이라
은총 있으리라

십자가 상 앞에 두 손 모아 성호 그으며
돈 보스꼬 안에서
우리 배우듯

멈추지 않는 역사의 수레바퀴 속에
형제들의 뜨거운 사랑
믿음과
봉사로
소망 이루어
평화동산 꽃피우는 등불이 되자
찬란한 역사의 주역이 되자

My Proud Brothers

At the golden waving plaza
You glory is brilliant
The light of divine grace is bright

Forty years have already passed since
We nested at the side of Mt. Taebong
In the southern region
Brothers warm heart and hot passion
Have made today's history
It is the day of deep emotion
It is also a glorious day
Diving grace dwells here

In Donbosco
As we had learned
We prayed before the cross statue

With continuing wheels of history
Brothers love is warm
With the wishes of faith and service
Let us be the lamps of flowery site of peace
Let us be the leaders of brilliant history

아!
21세기 닻을 올린
자랑스런 나의 형제여!
나의 살레시안이여!
영원히 영원히 축복있으라
영광 있으라

Ah!
You have weighed the anchor of the 21 century
My proud brothers!
My Salesians!
Eternally
God bless you eternally
Be glorious.

고황의 요람

고황산 기슭에 둥지를 틀고
청운의 꿈 가꿔온
형제들이여

산새들 다람쥐 쫓던
지난날의 얼킨 추억
삼삼오오 짝을 지어 거닐던
젊은날의 초상이
오늘 그대들의 가슴에
주마등으로 펼쳐지오니
마음껏 느끼소서
마음껏 누리소서

이 나라, 내 둥지
우리 손으로 가꾸자던
그대들의 열망
고황산 사자로 포효하더니
세계 향한 비상의 날개로
웅비의 장을 펼쳤구나

장하도다
거룩하도다
그대들의 힘찬 모습

The Cradle of Gowhang

Dear brothers
We had built a nest
At the foot of Mt. Gowhang
We had raise lofty ambitions

We had good old memories
We chased birds and squirrels
We used to walk by two and threes
The portrait of young days
Revolving lanterns of recollections
Are brought back to your heart today
Feel to the utmost
Enjoy as much as you please

This country is our nest
We have intended to embellish our nest
Your passion
You have howled as lions do
In the Mt. gowhang
You have spread the wings
To fly to the world

저, 시계탑 속에 쏟아지던 등불
반도를 비쳐
오대양 육대주를 밝히더니
인류가 우러르는 경희의 위상이여
그대들의 얼굴이여

피 끓는 그대들의 가슴
폭포수로 쏟아 붓고
대륙을 넘어 우주로
끝없이 끝없이 비상 하소서

그대들의 발자국 뒤엔
또 다른 형제들이 따르리니
영원 무궁 빛나리라
경희의 빛이여
경희의 위상이여

Your energetic features
Are praise worthy and sublime

The bright light of lanters in the clock tower
The light has lightend the Korea Peninsula
The five Oceans and Six continents
The world reveres the phase of Kyunghee
Noblesse oblige appears in your faces

You hearts are ardent
It's like a pouring water fall
Fly and fly endlessly
To the universe beyond the earth

The younger brothers follow your footprints
The light of Kyunghee will be radiant eternally
The noble phase of Kyunghee.

▌시인 약력 : 정찬우(鄭燦宇)

- 학력

  경희대학교 경영대학 경영학과 졸업
  서울대학교 경영대학원 졸업
  중앙대학교 국제경영대학원 졸업

- 경력

  현우트레이딩(주) 대표이사
  도서출판 밀레 대표이사
  (사) 한국수입협회 이사 역임
  (사)한국수입협회 문화예술위원장 역임
  (사)한국수입협회 부회장 역임
  (사)한국수입협회 자문단 의장
  밀레니엄문학회 회장
  (사)세계한민족 책사랑 무궁화 협회 이사장
  살레시안 연합회 부회장
  한국민족문학회 부회장
  (사)한국문인협회 저작권옹호위원
  (사)한국문인협회, 월간문학편집위원 역임
  (사)한국문인협회 이사 역임
  (사)한국문인협회 감사 역임
  (사)한국문인협회 자문위원
  (사)한국현대시인협회 중앙위원 역임
  (사)한국현대시인협회 이사, 기획위원 역임
  (사)국제펜한국본부 이사, 감사 역임
  (사)국제펜한국본부 자문위원
  KOIMA CEO 합창단 단장
  (사)서울오라토리오 합창단 단원
  (사)난파합창단 단원
  경희동문합창단 단원

About the Author : Chan Woo Chung, Poet

- Education ;
  - BA. ; College of Business Administration, Kyunghee University, Seoul
  - MBA. ; Graduate School of Business Administration Seoul National University
  - MBA. ; Graduate School of International Management Chung Ang University, Seoul

- Experiences ;
  - President of Hyun Woo Trading Co., Ltd.
  - President of the Mille Publishing Cmpany
  - Censor, former Trustee of Korea Importers Association(KOIMA)
  - Director of the Culture and Arts Committee of Korea Importers Association(KOIMA)
  - Forner Vice President of Korea Importers Association(KOIMA)
  - Chaiman of Consultant of Korea Importers Association (KOIMA)
  - Chaiman of the Society of Millennium Literature in Korea
  - Chaiman of the Association of Book love and Hibiscus Syracuse of Korea People in the World
  - Vice President of the Federation of the Korean Salesians
  - Vice President of the Association of Korea National Literature
  - Member of the Copyright Protection Committee of the Korea Writer's Association
  - Member of the Editorial of Monthly Literature Book in Korea Writer's Association
  - Trustee former of Korea Writers Association
  - Censor of Korea Writers Association
  - Consultant Member of Korea Writers Association
  - Central Committee of the Association of Modem Poets in Korea
  - Trustee, Committee of Planning Association of Modem Poets in Korea
  - Former Trustee and Censor of International PEN Korea
  - Consultant member of International PEN Korea Headquarters
  - Director of KOIMA CEO Chorus
  - Members of the Seoul Oratorio Chorus
  - Members of Nanpa Chorus
  - Members of Chrus KyungHee University

• 수상
부원문학상
한국민족문학상
탐미문학상
문학21문학상
에피포도문학상(미국)

• 저서
「다국적 기업의 다국적 마켓팅 전력」
「한국의 플렌트 수출 전략」

• 논문
「한국기업의 중국투자 진출에 관한 연구」
「한국의 중남미 전출 전략」 등 다수

• 자서전 대필
「전쟁과 우정」 정필기
「생동하는 삶은 역사다」 강두원

• 시집 (한 · 영대역시집)
「내 영혼의 하얀 미소」
「내게 사랑 하나 있네」
「꽃으로 선 당신」
「가끔은 이런 날이」
「황홀한 여정」
「하늘은 내게」
「달빛에 띄운 연정」
「회상의 날개」

- Literary Prizes ;
  - The Boowon Literature Prize
  - The Korea National Literature Prize
  - Tahmee Literary Prize
  - Literature 21 Prize
  - Epipodo Literary(U.S.A.)

- Books ;
  - Marketing Strategies of Multinations Enterprises
  - The Strategies of Export of Korea, and Others

- Articles ;
  - A Study of Investment in China
  - A Study of Investment in Middle and South Americas

- Biographies Review and slaboration (editorial supervision)
  - War & Friendship
  - The Viatal History of Living

- Korean-English Collection of Poems ;
  - *The Write Smile of my Soul*
  - *There is a Love for Me*
  - *You Stand Like A Flower*
  - *Sometimes This Day*
  - *A Fascinating Journey*
  - *The Heaven Is To Me*
  - *Love in the Moonlight*
  - *The Wings of Reminiscence*

번역자 약력 : 최홍규 (崔鴻圭)

영문학박사, 시인, 수필가, 문학평론가, 번역가(영어, 불어, 독어)
중앙대학교 영문학과 학사, 서울대학교 영어교육과 석사
동국대학교 영문학과 영문학박사

- 대학 경력
  중앙대학교 인문대학 교수, 명예교수
  미국 하버드대학, 예일대학, 풀브라이트 교환교수
  영국 케임브리지대학, 런던대학(UCL), 객원교수
  프랑스 파리IV대학(소르본대) 연구교수, 독일 뮌헨대학 초청교수

- 문학관련 경력
  한국문학종교학회장과 한국번역문학회장
  한국농민문학회장, 한국문인협회 문인복지위원
  한국문인협회 한국해외문학 발전위원,
  국제 PEN 한국본부 이사, 자문위원, 국제 PEN 재단 한국대표
  한국시인협회 상임, 중앙위원, 한국문화예술시인연대회장

- 수상
  미국 에피포도 문학상, 국제 PEN 번역문학상, 헤밍웨이문학상
  중앙대 문학상, 한국농민문학상, 동국대 동국문학상
  서울 서초문학상, 한국생활문학회 대상 국무총리 표창

- 포상(국가 훈장, 포장, 표창)
  황조근정훈장, 근정포장
  대통령표창, 국무총리표창

- 저서
  윌리엄 워즈워드의 자연관 외 12권
  학술논문 : 월트 휘트먼의 인간과 외 34편

- 번역서
  톰 존슨의 모험 ; 헨리필딩
  허영의 시장 ; 윌리엄 메이크피스 쌔커리,
  로버트 브라우닝 명시선, 위리엄 워즈의 명시선 외 15권
  정찬우 시집 ;「내 영혼의 하얀 미소」 외 7권

About the translator : HONGKYU Augustine CHOE

Education ; Chung-Ang University BA
Seoul National University MA
Dongguk University Ph D.

- Poet Essayist, Literary Critic, Translator
- Proficient in English, French, and German
- Professor, Professor emeritus ; Chung-Ang Unoversity, Seoul Korea

• Fullbright Exchange Professor ;
  - Yale University, Harvard University, USA
  - University of Cambridge, University of London UK
    Invited Professor
  - University of Paris IV (Sorbonne) France
  - Munchen University, German Visiting Professor

• President ; - The Korea Society for Literature and Religion
  - Pronotion Member of the Overseas Korea Literature of the Korea Writers Association
  - Committee of Welfare the Korea Writers Association ;
  - International PEN Foundation of Korea Represenrative
  - The Korea Poet's Association ; Standing Committee Member

• Awards ;
  - Epi-podo Award (English Poems, USA)
  - PEN Translation Award (Korea Center)
  - Hemingway Literary Award (Korea)
  - The Nongmin Literature Society of Korea

• National Doceration, Order, Commendation ;
  - Gounjeong Hunjang(drder), Geunjeong Pojang
  - President Commendation, Prime Minister Commendation

• Translator ; - Tom Jones by Henry Fielding
  - Vanity Fair by William Makepeace Thackeray
  - Selected Poems by Willam Wordswoth
  - A Fascinating Journey by Chan-Woo Chung and fifteen book
  - Translated 32 book of novel, essay

회상의 날개
The Wings of Reminiscence

인　쇄 | 2024년 3월 20일
발　행 | 2024년 3월 23일

지은이 | 정찬우
옮긴이 | 최홍규
펴낸곳 | 도서출판 밀레

등　록 | 2004년 12월 15일 제204078호
주　소 | 서울 서초구 효령로 53길 18, 210호
(서초동, 석탑오피스텔)
TEL : (02)588-4671~2
FAX : (02)588-4673
e-mail : hyunwoot@hanmail.net

값 20,000원
ISBN 978-89-97815-31-9